Audit of the Financial Stability Oversight Council's Compliance with Its Transparency Policy

Report to the Financial Stability Oversight Council and the Congress

Prepared by
The Council of Inspectors General
on Financial Oversight

July 2014

CIGFO-14-001

Table of Contents

Transmittal Letter 1
Executive Summary 3
Results of CIGFO Working Group Audit 6
    FSOC Complied With Its Transparency Policy 8
    Assessment of FSOC'S Transparency Policy 10
Conclusion And Recommendations 13
Appendices
    Appendix I: Objective, Scope, and Methodology 15
    Appendix II: October 2010 FSOC Transparency Policy 16
    Appendix III: May 2014 FSOC Transparency Policy 18
    Appendix IV: FSOC Response 20
    Appendix V: CIGFO Working Group 22

Abbreviations and Acronyms

CFPB	Consumer Financial Protection Bureau
CIGFO	Council of Inspectors General on Financial Oversight
Dodd-Frank Act	Dodd-Frank Wall Street Reform and Consumer Protection Act
FMU	financial market utility
FSOC or Council	Financial Stability Oversight Council
GAO	U.S. Government Accountability Office
MMF	money market fund
OFR	Office of Financial Research
OMB	Office of Management and Budget
Title I	Dodd-Frank Wall Street Reform and Consumer Protection Act, Title I—Financial Stability
Treasury	The Department of the Treasury

DEPARTMENT OF THE TREASURY
WASHINGTON, D.C. 20220

July 1, 2014

The Honorable Jacob J. Lew
Chair, Financial Stability Oversight Council
Washington, D.C. 20220

Dear Mr. Chairman:

I am pleased to present you with the Council of Inspectors General on Financial Oversight (CIGFO) audit report titled *Audit of the Financial Stability Oversight Council's Compliance with Its Transparency Policy.*

As its transparency policy is one of the Financial Stability Oversight Council's (FSOC) key governance documents, I proposed convening a working group to assess the Council's compliance with the transparency policy, and to determine if improvements could be made to the policy. The proposal was approved, and a CIGFO Working Group completed an audit.

In our report, we recommend that FSOC continue its efforts to (1) provide greater detail in the meeting minutes for closed meetings and (2) identify datasets and information that could be made publicly available; ensure such datasets and information are posted to its website, while continuing to protect market-sensitive or confidential information; and implement a permanent process for continuous, proactive identification, preparation and release of data on an ongoing basis.

I would like to take this opportunity to thank the FSOC members for their support, especially those Treasury officials who assisted with this effort.

CIGFO looks forward to working with you on this and other issues. In accordance with the Dodd-Frank Wall Street Reform and Consumer Protection Act, CIGFO is also providing this report to Congress.

Sincerely,

Eric M. Thorson
Chair
Council of Inspectors General on Financial Oversight

THIS PAGE IS INTENTIONALLY LEFT BLANK.

Executive Summary

Why and How We Conducted this Audit

The Dodd-Frank Wall Street Reform and Consumer Protection Act (Dodd-Frank Act) created a comprehensive regulatory and resolution framework designed to reduce the severe economic consequences of economic instability. The Dodd-Frank Act established the Financial Stability Oversight Council (FSOC or Council) and charged it with identifying risks to the nation's financial stability, promoting market discipline, and responding to emerging threats to the stability of the nation's financial system. Among other things, Title I of the Dodd-Frank Act (Title I) requires the Council to meet at least quarterly. On October 1, 2010, at its first meeting, FSOC voted to approve a transparency policy that pertains to the openness and transparency of its meetings.

The Dodd-Frank Act also established the Council of Inspectors General on Financial Oversight (CIGFO). CIGFO's statutory functions include oversight of FSOC. In this regard, the law authorizes CIGFO to convene a working group, by a majority vote, for the purpose of evaluating the effectiveness and internal operations of FSOC. In September 2013, Eric Thorson, CIGFO Chair and Department of the Treasury (Treasury) Inspector General, proposed convening a working group to assess the extent to which FSOC is operating in a manner consistent with expectations outlined in its transparency policy, and to consider whether improvements to FSOC's transparency policy could be made. CIGFO approved the proposal and formed a Working Group.

To accomplish its objective, the CIGFO Working Group conducted a review of FSOC's transparency policy and tested whether FSOC was compliant with its own policy. The working group also assessed FSOC's transparency policy by analyzing laws, directives, and other organizations' policies or practices related to transparency. Appendix I provides a more detailed description of the working group's objective, scope, and methodology.

What We Learned

Based on our review of documents from October 2010 through December 2013, we determined FSOC operated in a manner consistent with the expectations outlined in its transparency policy. Specifically, FSOC:

- held at least two open meetings each year;
- made all open meetings available to the public via a live web stream;
- released minutes of each meeting;
- recorded all votes of Council members in the meeting minutes;
- voted on proposed and final rules during open meetings; and
- reported on its compliance with the transparency policy in its annual report to Congress.

FSOC's transparency policy outlined eight specific reasons why a meeting or portion of a meeting could be closed, and stated that the decision to close a meeting is determined by the Chairperson based on the agenda, or upon an affirmative vote of a majority of the voting members. However, when a meeting or portion thereof was closed, we found that FSOC did not inform the public which of the eight reasons applied to the determination.

While we concluded that FSOC complied with its transparency policy, we identified practices in place during the time of our fieldwork related to meetings that, if incorporated into the policy, would make it stronger. Specifically, the policy did not include FSOC's practices of (1) posting public notices for upcoming meetings to its website 7 days in advance of a regularly scheduled meeting, (2) issuing a press readout upon completion of Council meetings, and (3) posting minutes to its website immediately following approval.

We also identified certain additional practices that FSOC should implement to increase transparency: (1) providing more detailed minutes for closed meetings, while protecting market-sensitive or confidential information; (2) posting meeting agendas to its website in advance of Council meetings; and (3) identifying additional data and information that could be made available to the public and posting such data and information to its website. By doing these things, we believe FSOC will enhance public confidence in the accountability and integrity of Council activities.

On May 7, 2014, subsequent to the completion of our fieldwork, FSOC unanimously approved a revised transparency policy. Work on this revised transparency policy started before our audit and considered matters we brought to the attention of FSOC staff during the audit. The revised policy includes the following new provisions: (1) providing not less than 7 days advance notice of any regularly scheduled meeting on its website, including information about the agenda, the reason(s) for closing a meeting, if applicable, and the time and place of any open meeting; (2) as soon as practicable after each meeting, making information about the meeting available on FSOC's website; and (3) when practicable, releasing meeting minutes immediately following the next regularly scheduled meeting. The revised policy also includes a ninth specific reason why a meeting or portion of a meeting could be closed. See appendix II for FSOC's October 2010 transparency policy and appendix III for the May 2014 revised transparency policy.

In considering our recommendations to FSOC, we also note recent concerns expressed by certain Members of Congress about the transparency of FSOC's activities.

Recommendations

We acknowledge FSOC's efforts to improve its transparency through its revised transparency policy. We recommend the Council continue its efforts to (1) provide greater detail in the meeting minutes for closed meetings and (2) identify datasets and information that could be made publicly available; ensure such datasets and information are posted to its website, while continuing to protect market-sensitive or confidential information; and implement a permanent process for continuous, proactive identification, preparation and release of data on an ongoing basis.

FSOC Response

In a written response, FSOC stated that the Council has recognized the importance of transparency since its first meeting in 2010, when it voluntarily adopted a transparency policy. Since then, the Council has considered how to open up more of its work to the public, while at the same time respecting its need to discuss supervisory and other market-sensitive data, including information about individual firms, transactions, and markets that require confidentiality. As the CIGFO report noted, Council staff had already begun, before the CIGFO review started, a broad review of the Council's governance practices, including its transparency policy, to identify ways to further strengthen the Council's commitment to openness. As a result of this internal review, the Council voted in an open session on May 7, 2014, to adopt enhancements to its transparency policy.

With respect to the recommendation to provide greater detail in the meeting minutes for closed meetings, the Council is fully committed to maintaining the practice of incorporating additional detail in its minutes, while still protecting the confidentiality of market-sensitive or supervisory information that are often the subject of Council discussions. With respect to the recommendation to identify datasets and information that could be made publicly available, FSOC noted that it already provides on its website a significant amount of information. Also, as a collaborative body that brings together the independent financial regulators, much of the data relied upon by the Council is provided by those agencies and the Office of Financial Research, which maintain the responsibility for determining whether to make their data available to the public. However, to the extent that the Council considers data and information during Council meetings, Council staff will routinely evaluate whether such materials could be made available to the public, in light of any applicable confidentiality restrictions.

CIGFO Working Group Comments

We consider FSOC's commitments and planned actions responsive to our recommendations. We recognize that the Council considers market-sensitive and confidential data and information from multiple entities. To the extent FSOC staff identifies materials that could be made public, the Council should ensure those materials are posted to its website in a timely manner.

Results of CIGFO Working Group Audit

Introduction

In 2010, FSOC approved a transparency policy intended to provide for openness and transparency of Council meetings.[1] This report presents the results of the CIGFO Working Group's audit of FSOC's compliance with its transparency policy. This is the third audit that a CIGFO Working Group has issued to the Council and the Congress as part of CIGFO's responsibility to oversee FSOC under the Dodd-Frank Act. CIGFO issued its first two audits in June 2012[2] and July 2013.[3]

Background

The Dodd-Frank Act established FSOC to create joint accountability for identifying and mitigating potential threats to the stability of the nation's financial system. By creating FSOC, Congress recognized that protecting financial stability would require the collective engagement of the entire financial regulatory community. As shown in the following table, FSOC consists of 10 voting members and 5 nonvoting members and brings together the expertise of federal financial regulators, state regulators, and an insurance expert appointed by the President with Senate confirmation.

Table 1: FSOC Membership	
Federal and Independent Members	**State Members**
• Secretary of the Treasury, Chairperson (v)	• State Insurance Commissioner
• Chairman of the Board of Governors of the Federal Reserve System (v)	• State Banking Supervisor
• Comptroller of the Currency (v)	• State Securities Commissioner
• Director of the Consumer Financial Protection Bureau (v)	
• Chairman of the Securities and Exchange Commission (v)	
• Chairperson of the Federal Deposit Insurance Corporation (v)	
• Chairperson of the Commodity Futures Trading Commission (v)	
• Director of the Federal Housing Finance Agency (v)	
• Chairman of the National Credit Union Administration Board (v)	
• Director of the Office of Financial Research	
• Director of the Federal Insurance Office	
• Independent member with insurance expertise (v)	
(v) Indicates Voting Member	

---

[1] Title I requires the Council to meet at least quarterly.

[2] CIGFO, *Audit of the Financial Stability Oversight Council's Controls over Non-public Information*, (June 22, 2012)

[3] CIGFO, *Audit of the Financial Stability Oversight Council's Designation of Financial Market Utilities*, (July 12, 2013)

The purposes of FSOC are to:

- identify risks to the financial stability of the U.S. that could arise from the material financial distress or failure, or ongoing activities, of large, interconnected bank holding companies or nonbank financial companies, or that could arise outside the financial services marketplace;

- promote market discipline, by eliminating expectations on the part of shareholders, creditors, and counterparties of such companies that the U.S. Government will shield them from losses in the event of failure; and

- respond to emerging threats to the stability of the U.S. financial system.

Within Treasury, a dedicated policy office, led by a Deputy Assistant Secretary, functions as the FSOC Secretariat and serves as a mechanism to bring issues to the Council through a coordinated process. The voting members of FSOC provide a federal regulatory perspective as well as an independent insurance expert's view. The nonvoting members offer different insights as state-level representatives from bank, securities, and insurance regulators or as the directors of offices within Treasury – the Office of Financial Research and the Federal Insurance Office.

FSOC Secretariat staff developed a transparency policy in 2010 with input from FSOC member agencies. On October 1, 2010, at its first meeting, the Council voted on and unanimously approved the policy. The policy was intended to provide for transparency of Council meetings. The transparency policy is provided as Appendix II.

FSOC Secretariat staff told us they recently reviewed the Council's governance framework, including its transparency policy, to identify potential improvements. These potential improvements included (1) revising the policy to formally adopt the practice of posting notices to FSOC's website for upcoming meetings at least 7 days in advance, when possible; (2) including in the notices a high-level, preliminary agenda for each meeting, and the time and place of open meetings; (3) requiring the posting of a statement with basic information to FSOC's website after each Council meeting (prior to the meeting minutes being available); and (4) providing additional detail in meeting minutes while protecting market-sensitive or confidential information.

Audit Approach

Our audit objective was to assess the extent to which FSOC is operating in a manner consistent with the expectations outlined in its transparency policy. Our audit scope included the period from October 2010 through December 2013. We also considered whether improvements to FSOC's transparency policy could be made.

To accomplish our objective, we reviewed relevant FSOC records to determine compliance with its transparency policy. In addition, participating Offices of Inspector General collected information from FSOC federal members regarding FSOC's transparency policy and practices. We collected similar information from the FSOC Secretariat and FSOC non-federal members. Furthermore, we reviewed laws, directives, and other organizations' policies or practices relevant to transparency.

We conducted our audit fieldwork from January through March 2014 in accordance with generally accepted government auditing standards. We provided an exit briefing on the overall results of our work to FSOC representatives on May 8, 2014.

FSOC COMPLIED WITH ITS TRANSPARENCY POLICY

We determined that FSOC complied with its October 2010 transparency policy. The policy requirements and what we found are described below.

Hold two open meetings each year

FSOC's transparency policy committed FSOC to holding two open meetings each year. We determined that from October 2010 through December 2013, the Council met 36 times, either in person (27) or telephonically (9).[4] Of the 27 meetings held in person, 11 meetings included a portion that was open to the public via a live web stream. As shown below, FSOC held at least two open meetings each year.

- 2010 – 2 open meetings
- 2011 – 4 open meetings
- 2012 – 3 open meetings
- 2013 – 2 open meetings

Open meetings to the press and public via a live web stream

The policy stated that FSOC will make its meetings open to the press and to the public via a live web stream except when supervisory and market-sensitive information is being discussed and for certain other enumerated reasons. Council meetings were either closed entirely or consisted of closed and open sessions. If a meeting consisted of both types of sessions, the closed session was held first, followed by the open session.

We determined that for each of the 11 meetings that included a portion open to the public, there was a live web stream made available for that portion of the meeting. Videos of all 11 web streams are maintained on FSOC's website.

Minutes of meetings

The policy stated that FSOC will release meeting minutes after each meeting, and that the minutes are subject to redactions, as determined by the Chairperson. We determined that minutes were (1) prepared for each of the 36 Council meetings, (2) approved at the next meeting, and (3) posted to FSOC's website within a day of being approved.

FSOC does not keep detailed transcripts of Council meetings. An FSOC Secretariat official stated that the meeting minutes are sufficient for the needs of the Council and serve as the Council's internal record. This official also stated that there have not been any redactions to the meeting minutes, although in some

---

[4] These FSOC meetings conducted by conference call were held to discuss single-issue emerging matters that could impact the financial sector.

instances, certain sensitive materials attached to the minutes as appendices have been omitted from the minutes posted on FSOC's website.

Votes of Council members

The transparency policy stated that all votes of Council members will be recorded and reflected in the minutes of the Council. In addition to votes to approve meeting minutes and annual reports, examples of votes included resolutions to appoint the Chairperson of the Deputies Committee, Rules of Organization of the Council, and various proposed and final rules. We determined that for all scheduled Council votes (i.e., votes included as agenda items), the results of the votes were recorded in the minutes of the corresponding Council meetings.

Votes on proposed or final rules

FSOC's policy stated that when FSOC members are asked to vote on a draft FSOC proposed or final rule, FSOC will make those agenda items open to the public. We determined that FSOC members voted on nine proposed or final rules, and all of the votes were conducted during the open portion of the meetings.

Reporting compliance with transparency policy

FSOC's transparency policy stated that, as part of FSOC's annual report to Congress, it will report on its compliance with its transparency policy. We determined that FSOC's 2011 through 2014 annual reports to Congress stated that FSOC complied with its transparency policy.

Opening or closing of Council meetings

The transparency policy stated that meetings will be open or may be closed, in whole or in part, as determined by the Chairperson based on the agenda, or upon an affirmative vote of a majority of the voting members. The reasons that a meeting or portion thereof would be closed included circumstances where holding an open meeting could:

1. result in the disclosure of information contained in or related to investigation, examination, operating, or condition reports prepared by, on behalf of, or for the use of, an agency responsible for the regulation or supervision of financial markets or financial institutions;

2. result in the disclosure of information that would lead to significant financial speculation, significantly endanger the stability of any financial market or financial institution, or significantly frustrate implementation of a proposed agency action;

3. result in the disclosure of information exempted from disclosure by statute or by regulation; or authorized under criteria established by an Executive Order to be kept secret;

4. result in the disclosure of trade secrets and commercial or financial information obtained from a person and privileged or confidential;

5. result in the disclosure of information of a personal nature that would constitute an unwarranted invasion of personal privacy or be inconsistent with Federal privacy laws, or the disclosure of information that relates solely to internal personnel rules or practices;

6. result in the disclosure of investigatory records compiled for law enforcement or supervisory purposes;

7. result in the disclosure of inter-agency or intra-agency memoranda or letters that would not otherwise be available by law; or

8. necessarily and significantly compromise the mission or purposes of the FSOC, as determined by the Chairman with the concurrence of a majority of the voting member agencies or by a majority of the voting member agencies.

We reviewed the agendas and meeting minutes for all 36 Council meetings held from October 2010 through December 2013, and found no mention of the specific reason why a meeting or portion of a meeting was closed. Nevertheless, based on our review of the minutes from the closed meetings, we were able to link the discussions documented in the minutes to one or more of the reasons for closure listed above.

When asked about the decision-making process on whether to close a Council meeting, FSOC Secretariat personnel told us that typically 2 weeks in advance of each meeting, the FSOC Deputies Committee[5] considers potential Council meeting agendas and whether the meetings should be open or closed. Based on the consensus of the FSOC Deputies Committee, FSOC Secretariat staff prepare and send the Chairperson and all other Council members a copy of the proposed agenda that indicates whether each agenda item is proposed for discussion in an open or closed session in advance of each Council meeting. According to FSOC Secretariat personnel, to date, the Chairperson has accepted all the Deputies Committee's proposals and no Council votes have occurred on the subject of opening or closing a meeting.

On May 7, 2014, subsequent to the completion of our fieldwork, FSOC unanimously approved a revised transparency policy. Among other things, the revised policy includes a new provision that states FSOC will provide not less than 7 days advance notice of any regularly scheduled meeting on its website, including information about the reason(s) for closing a meeting, if applicable. We believe this new provision will enhance FSOC's transparency.

ASSESSMENT OF FSOC'S TRANSPARENCY POLICY

FSOC's transparency policy did not incorporate current practices

FSOC's transparency policy focused on the transparency of Council meetings. While we concluded that FSOC complied with its transparency policy, we identified key FSOC practices related to meetings that were not incorporated into the policy. These practices are discussed below and were separately identified by the FSOC Secretariat staff and the FSOC Deputies Committee as potential revisions to the Council's transparency policy.

We noted that FSOC's practices included posting public notices for upcoming meetings on its website 7 days in advance of a regularly scheduled meeting. These notices provided the date of the meeting, whether the meeting would be open or closed and, when applicable, the expected start time for the open session. Soon after each meeting, the meeting notice was removed from FSOC's website and replaced with language notifying the public that the meeting had occurred. FSOC's practices also included providing a press readout to the media after each meeting held in closed session, which included a high level description of the

---

[5] The Deputies Committee coordinates and oversees the work of the interagency staff committees and is made up of senior officials representing each FSOC member.

meeting. We noted that the transparency policy did not require providing public notifications of regularly scheduled upcoming Council meetings or press readouts to the media. We also noted FSOC did not post the information from these press readouts to its website. The May 2014 revised policy includes the following new provisions: (1) providing not less than 7 days advance notice of any regularly scheduled meeting on its website, including the time and place of any open meeting; and (2) as soon as practicable after each meeting, making information about the meeting available on FSOC's website. We believe these new provisions address our concerns that the transparency policy did not include key practices related to FSOC meetings, and that FSOC did not post information about its meetings to its website soon after the meetings.

The October 2010 transparency policy stated that FSOC will release minutes of meetings after each meeting, but did not specify when the minutes would be released. The May 2014 transparency policy specifies that when practicable, the Council will release its meeting minutes immediately following the next regularly scheduled meeting. We believe the new policy gives more specificity about when the meeting minutes will be released.

FSOC should increase the level of detail in its closed meeting minutes

As noted earlier, the majority of FSOC meetings were closed to the public. Meeting minutes for closed meetings give general information about agenda items and presenters. Discussion in the minutes of specific agenda items is high-level and lacks detail. We noted that in some instances, portions of agenda item topics were already in the public domain; therefore those portions could have been covered more fully in meeting minutes. For example, during the closed session of a meeting on December 9, 2013, the Director of the Consumer Financial Protection Bureau (CFPB) gave a presentation on certain CFPB housing finance rules. The meeting minutes stated that the Director provided an overview of the ability-to-repay/qualified mortgage rule and also presented on the servicing rules, which apply to both banks and nonbanks, and were to take effect on January 10, 2014. Because the rules were final and publicly available, FSOC could have included more details about the presentation in its meeting minutes.

In our July 12, 2013 audit, we noted that during the financial market utilities (FMU) designation process, FSOC identified certain foreign-based FMUs as potential candidates for designation as systemically important. However, FSOC decided not to consider possible designation at the time pending further deliberations.[6] According to the FSOC Secretariat, this matter was, and continues to be, still under review. We reviewed FSOC meeting minutes and annual reports and did not find any mention of this matter. We believe that because this information is important, FSOC should have included it in its meeting minutes.

In a September 2012 report, the U.S. Government Accountability Office (GAO) noted the lack of detail in FSOC's closed meeting minutes, and how this made it difficult to assess FSOC's performance.[7] Since that GAO report, meeting minutes for some closed agenda items have improved. For example, the October 11, 2011, meeting included an agenda item on money market fund (MMF) reform. The meeting minutes noted that a presentation was given that covered actions taken since the last time MMF reform was before the Council,

---

[6] CIGFO, *Audit of the Financial Stability Oversight Council's Designation of Financial Market Utilities*, page 12.

[7] GAO, *Financial Stability: New Council and Research Office Should Strengthen the Accountability and Transparency of Their Decisions* (GAO12886; Sept. 2012). In the report, GAO stated that minutes describe general agenda items for the meetings and information on the presenters for each agenda item and lack additional detail. GAO recommended that FSOC keep detailed minutes of closed sessions.

the reform options under consideration, and next steps, but no further details were provided. In contrast, the meeting minutes for a July 16, 2013, meeting with another MMF reform agenda item contained greater detail about a presentation on a proposed rule for MMF reform. The minutes explained that the proposed rule set forth two alternatives for amending the rules that govern MMFs and contained the details of the new requirements each alternative would impose on MMFs.

While we have seen some improvement in the level of detail included in the minutes for closed Council meetings, the December 9, 2013, meeting minutes regarding a presentation on certain CFPB housing finance rules described above indicates that there is still room for improvement. While we agree that closed meetings are required for discussions of supervisory and other market-sensitive data, there may be information and presentations from closed meetings that do not contain supervisory or market-sensitive data. FSOC should as a practice include this information for all agenda items in its meeting minutes.

FSOC did not make meeting agendas available to the public on its website

As discussed earlier, FSOC's Deputies Committee considers potential Council meeting agendas typically 2 weeks before each meeting, and FSOC posts meeting notices to its website at least 7 days in advance, when possible. However, FSOC did not post meeting agendas to its website. Two FSOC members stated that posting meeting agendas would improve FSOC's transparency. As previously mentioned, FSOC Secretariat personnel identified providing high-level, preliminary agendas to the public before each meeting as potentially improving its transparency. We note that the May 2014 transparency policy includes a new provision that provides for not less than 7 days advance notice of any regularly scheduled meeting on its website, including information about the meeting agenda. We believe this new provision addresses our concern the FSOC was not posting meeting agendas on its website.

FSOC should continue to identify datasets and information to make available to the public

FSOC is subject to the Office of Management and Budget (OMB) Memorandum M-10-06, Open Government Directive.[8] According to an FSOC Secretariat official, FSOC complies with the directive through Treasury's Open Government Plan.[9] In its Open Government Plan, Treasury has committed to identifying current datasets and information to make available to the public and implementing a permanent process for continuous, proactive identification, preparation and release of data on an ongoing basis. We noted that following its designations of FMUs and nonbank financial companies, FSOC posted information supporting these designations on its website and in its annual reports. FSOC also included significant amounts of economic and financial information in its annual reports, and posted the corresponding datasets on its website. In the future, to the extent that FSOC considers datasets and information during Council meetings, FSOC should (1) identify which of those datasets and information could be made available to the public, and ensure the identified datasets and information are posted to FSOC's website; and (2) implement an ongoing

---

[8] Issued in December 2009, the OMB Memorandum directs executive departments and agencies to take specific actions to implement the principles of transparency, participation, and collaboration, including developing an Open Government Plan that describes how it will improve transparency and integrate public participation and collaboration into its activities.

[9] Department of the Treasury Open Government Plan 2.1, September 2012

process for continuous, proactive identification, preparation, and release of data. We believe this is important to meet the objectives of the Open Government Directive.

Conclusion and Recommendations

We determined that FSOC complied with its transparency policy. However, when a Council meeting or portion thereof was closed, FSOC did not inform the public which of eight possible reasons for closing the meeting applied. In addition, FSOC's transparency policy did not require FSOC's practices of (1) posting public notices for upcoming meetings to its website 7 days in advance of a regularly scheduled meeting, (2) issuing a press readout upon completion of Council meetings, and (3) approving meeting minutes and then posting minutes to its website immediately following the approvals. We also identified certain practices that FSOC should improve upon or implement to increase transparency, namely (1) providing greater detail in minutes for closed meetings, while protecting market-sensitive or confidential information; (2) posting meeting agendas to its website in advance of Council meetings; and (3) continuing to identify datasets and information that could be made available to the public and posting it to its website.

On May 7, 2014, after we completed our fieldwork, FSOC approved a revised transparency policy. The revised policy includes the following new provisions: (1) providing not less than 7 days advance notice of any regularly scheduled meeting on its website, including information about the agenda, the reasons for closing a meeting, if applicable, and the time and place of any open meeting; (2) as soon as practicable after each meeting, making information about the meeting available on its website; and (3) when practicable, releasing meeting minutes immediately following the next regularly scheduled meeting.

In considering our recommendations below, we also note recent concern expressed by certain Members of Congress about the transparency of FSOC's activities. For example, H.R. 4387, the FSOC Transparency and Accountability Act, was proposed on April 3, 2014, that would, among other things, make FSOC subject to the Government in the Sunshine Act.[10] While the fate of this legislation is unknown at this time, it does underscore the need for FSOC to maintain its commitment to transparency. Accordingly, while we acknowledge FSOC's efforts to improve its transparency through its revised policy, we recommend the Council continue its efforts in the following areas.

1. Provide greater detail in the meeting minutes for closed meetings.

    FSOC Response

    Recent minutes of Council meetings have already begun to incorporate greater detail. This increased detail is the result of the Council's effort to provide the public with as much information as possible about its confidential deliberations, while still protecting the confidentiality of market-sensitive or supervisory information that are often the subject of Council discussions. The Council is fully committed to maintaining this practice of incorporating additional detail in its minutes.

---

[10] Codified as 5 USC 552b, this act prescribes that except as provided in the statute, every portion of every meeting of an agency shall be open to public observation. There are 10 exceptions to this requirement, including 2 exceptions related to sensitive financial institution information.

CIGFO Working Group Comment

FSOC's commitment to incorporating additional detail in its meeting minutes is responsive to our recommendation.

2. In the future, to the extent that FSOC considers datasets and information during Council meetings, identify datasets and information that it could make publicly available; ensure such datasets and information are posted to its website, while continuing to protect market-sensitive or confidential information; and implement a permanent process for continuous, proactive identification, preparation and release of data on an ongoing basis.

FSOC Response

The Council already provides on its website a significant amount of information, including financial and economic data used in the preparation of its annual reports and information about the basis for each of its designations of financial market utilities and nonbank financial companies. As a collaborative body that brings together the independent financial regulators, much of the data relied upon by the Council is provided by those agencies and the Office of Financial Research, which maintain the responsibility for determining whether to make their data available to the public. However, to the extent that the Council considers data and information during Council meetings, Council staff will routinely evaluate whether such materials could be made available to the public, in light of any applicable confidentiality restrictions.

CIGFO Working Group Comment

FSOC's commitment to routinely evaluate materials it considers for potential public disclosure is responsive to our recommendation. We recognize that the Council considers market-sensitive and confidential data and information from multiple entities. To the extent FSOC staff identifies materials that could be made public, the Council should ensure those materials are posted to its website in a timely manner.

Appendix I: Objective, Scope, and Methodology

Objective

The audit objective was to assess the extent to which the Financial Stability Oversight Council (FSOC or Council) is operating in a manner consistent with expectations outlined in its transparency policy, and to consider whether improvements to FSOC's transparency policy could be made.

Scope and Methodology

The scope of this audit included the FSOC meetings from October 2010 through December 2013.

To accomplish our objective, we:

- reviewed FSOC's transparency policy, Council meeting minutes, Council meeting agendas, meeting webcasts, FSOC's website, FSOC's annual reports, and other documentation provided by the FSOC Secretariat;
- interviewed officials of the FSOC Secretariat and FSOC member agencies;
- reviewed and analyzed laws, directives, and other organizations' transparency policies and practices; and
- compared other organizations' transparency policies, practices and websites to FSOC's transparency policy and website.

The organizations included in our review were the Millennium Challenge Corporation, International Monetary Fund, the Federal Reserve System's Federal Open Market Committee, Federal Deposit Insurance Corporation, Federal Financial Institutions Examination Council, Department of the Treasury, and the General Services Administration.

We performed audit fieldwork from January through March 2014. We conducted this performance audit in accordance with generally accepted government auditing standards. Those standards require that we plan and perform the audit to obtain sufficient, appropriate evidence to provide a reasonable basis for our findings and conclusions based on our audit objective. We believe that the evidence obtained provides a reasonable basis for our findings and conclusions based on our audit objective.

Appendix II: October 2010 FSOC Transparency Policy

Transparency Policy for the Financial Stability Oversight Council

The Financial Stability Oversight Council ("FSOC") was established by the Dodd-Frank Wall Street Reform and Consumer Protection Act ("Dodd-Frank Act").

The FSOC is committed to conducting its business in an open and transparent manner. Accordingly, the FSOC will make its meetings open to the press and to the public via a live web stream, except as necessary in the circumstances described below. The FSOC will also release minutes of meetings after each meeting. Minutes are subject to redactions, as determined by the Chairperson. As part of its annual report to Congress under the Dodd-Frank Act (§112(a)(2)(N)), the FSOC will report on compliance with its transparency policy.

The FSOC will open its meetings to the public whenever possible. At the same time, the central mission of the FSOC is to monitor systemic and emerging threats. This will require discussion of supervisory and other market-sensitive data, including information about individual firms, transactions, and markets that may only be obtained if maintained on a confidential basis. Protection of this information will be necessary in order to prevent destabilizing market speculation that could occur if that information were to be disclosed.

Accordingly, meetings will be open or may be closed, in whole or in part, as determined by the Chairperson based on the agenda, or upon an affirmative vote of a majority of the voting members. An FSOC member may request a vote on a decision of the Chairperson to close a meeting in whole or in part. The FSOC commits to holding two open meetings each year. In addition, when FSOC Members are asked to vote on a draft of an FSOC proposed or final rule, the FSOC will make those agenda items open to the public. All votes of Council members will be recorded and reflected in the minutes of the Council.

The reasons that a meeting or portion thereof would be closed include circumstances where holding an open meeting could:

- result in the disclosure of information contained in or related to investigation, examination, operating, or condition reports prepared by, on behalf of, or for the use of, an agency responsible for the regulation or supervision of financial markets or financial institutions;
- result in the disclosure of information which would lead to significant financial speculation, significantly endanger the stability of any financial

market or financial institution, or significantly frustrate implementation of a proposed agency action;
- result in the disclosure of information exempted from disclosure by statute or by regulation; or authorized under criteria established by an Executive Order to be kept secret;
- result in the disclosure of trade secrets and commercial or financial information obtained from a person and privileged or confidential;
- result in the disclosure of information of a personal nature that would constitute an unwarranted invasion of personal privacy or be inconsistent with Federal privacy laws, or of information that relates solely to internal personnel rules or practices;
- result in the disclosure of investigatory records compiled for law enforcement or supervisory purposes;
- result in the disclosure of inter-agency or intra-agency memoranda or letters which would not otherwise be available by law; or
- necessarily and significantly compromise the mission or purposes of the FSOC, as determined by the Chairman with the concurrence of a majority of the voting member agencies or by a majority of the voting member agencies.

Appendix III: May 2014 FSOC Transparency Policy

Transparency Policy for the Financial Stability Oversight Council

The Financial Stability Oversight Council ("Council") was established by the Dodd-Frank Wall Street Reform and Consumer Protection Act ("Dodd-Frank Act").

The Council is committed to conducting its business in an open and transparent manner. The Council will open its meetings to the public whenever possible. At the same time, the central mission of the Council is to monitor systemic and emerging threats. This will require discussion of supervisory and other market-sensitive data, including information about individual firms, transactions, and markets that may only be obtained if maintained on a confidential basis. Protection of this information will be necessary in order to prevent destabilizing market speculation that could occur if that information were to be disclosed. As part of its annual report to Congress under the Dodd-Frank Act (§ 112(a)(2)(N)), the Council will report on compliance with its transparency policy.

Council meetings may be open or closed, in whole or in part, based on the agenda and the reasons described below, as determined by the Chairperson or by an affirmative vote of a majority of the voting members. A Council member may request a vote on a decision of the Chairperson to open or close a meeting in whole or in part. The Council commits to holding at least two open meetings each year. In addition, when the Council is asked to vote on a draft of a Council proposed or final rule, the Council will make those agenda items open to the public.

The Council will provide not less than seven days' advance notice of any regularly scheduled meeting on its website, including information about the agenda, the reasons for closing a meeting, if applicable, and the time and place of any open meeting. The Council will make its open meetings open to the press and to the public via a live web stream. As soon as practicable after each meeting, the Council will make information about the meeting available on its website. The Council will also release minutes of meetings. All votes of Council members will be recorded and reflected in the minutes of the Council. When practicable, the Council will release its minutes immediately following its next regularly scheduled meeting. Minutes may be subject to redactions, as determined by the Chairperson.

The reasons that a meeting or portion thereof would be closed include circumstances where holding an open meeting could:

- result in the disclosure of information contained in or related to investigation, examination, operating, or condition reports prepared by, on behalf of, or for the use of, an agency responsible for the regulation or supervision of financial markets or financial institutions;

- result in the disclosure of information which would lead to significant financial speculation, significantly endanger the stability of any financial market or financial institution, or significantly frustrate implementation of a proposed agency action;

- result in the disclosure of information exempted from disclosure by statute or by regulation, or authorized under criteria established by an Executive Order to be kept secret;

- result in the disclosure of trade secrets and commercial or financial information obtained from a person and privileged or confidential;

- result in the disclosure of information of a personal nature that would constitute an unwarranted invasion of personal privacy or be inconsistent with Federal privacy laws, or of information that relates solely to internal personnel rules or practices;

- result in the disclosure of investigatory records compiled for law enforcement or supervisory purposes;

- result in the disclosure of inter-agency or intra-agency memoranda or letters which would not otherwise be available by law;

- involve the conduct solely of administrative business of the Council; or

- necessarily and significantly compromise the mission or purposes of the Council, as determined by the Chairperson with the concurrence of a majority of the voting members or by a majority of the voting members.

Source: FSOC website,
http://www.treasury.gov/initiatives/fsoc/Documents/The%20Council%27s%20Transparency%20Policy.pdf

Appendix IV: FSOC Response

DEPARTMENT OF THE TREASURY
WASHINGTON, D.C.

UNDER SECRETARY

May 30, 2014

The Honorable Eric M. Thorson
Chair, Council of Inspectors General
on Financial Oversight (CIGFO)
1500 Pennsylvania Avenue, NW
Washington, D.C. 20220

Re: Response to CIGFO's Draft Audit Report *Audit of the Financial Stability Oversight Council's Compliance with Its Transparency Policy*

Dear Mr. Chairman:

Thank you for the opportunity to review and respond to your draft audit report, *Audit of the Financial Stability Oversight Council's Compliance with Its Transparency Policy*, dated May 2014 (the Draft Report). The Financial Stability Oversight Council (Council) and its members and member agencies appreciate the CIGFO working group's review of the Council's adherence to its transparency policy. This letter responds, on behalf of the Secretary of the Treasury as Chairperson of the Council, to the Draft Report. The staffs of Council members and member agencies previously provided comments and technical suggestions to CIGFO staff.

CIGFO found that the Council fully complied with its transparency policy, including by holding two or more open meetings per year; by making those meeting available to the public via a live and archived web stream; by releasing minutes for all of its meetings within a day of approval; by recording all Council votes in meeting minutes; by voting on all proposed and final rules at meetings that are open to the public; and by opening or closing Council meetings based on the reasons described in the transparency policy.

The Council has recognized the importance of transparency since its first meeting in 2010, when it voluntarily adopted a transparency policy. Since then, the Council has considered how to open up more of its work to the public, while at the same time respecting its need to discuss supervisory and other market-sensitive data, including information about individual firms, transactions, and markets that require confidentiality. As the Draft Report notes, before the beginning of CIGFO's review, the Council's staff had already begun a broad review of the Council's governance practices, including its transparency policy, to identify ways to further strengthen the Council's commitment to openness. As a result of this internal review, on May 7, 2014, the Council voted in an open session to adopt enhancements to its transparency policy, as well as bylaws for its Deputies Committee. Those actions were based on the internal review but addressed many of the same improvements identified by CIGFO's working group during its field work. The transparency practices formally adopted by the Council included providing public notice on its website at least seven days before all regularly scheduled meetings; providing preliminary information about the agenda in the notice for each upcoming meeting; and posting to our website immediately after each meeting information about that meeting in advance of the release of formal meeting minutes

The Draft Report also makes two recommendations. First, the Draft Report recommends that the Council continue to provide greater detail in its meeting minutes for closed meetings. As the Draft Report notes, recent minutes of Council meetings have already begun to incorporate greater detail. This increased detail is the result of the Council's effort to provide the public with as much information as possible about its confidential deliberations, while still protecting the confidentiality of market-sensitive or supervisory information that are often the subject of Council discussions. The Council is fully committed to maintaining this practice of incorporating additional detail in its minutes.

Second, the Draft Report recommends that the Council identify datasets and information that it could make publically available; ensure such datasets and information are posted to its website, while continuing to protect market-sensitive or confidential information; and implement a permanent process for continuous, proactive identification, preparation and release of data on an ongoing basis. As noted in the Draft Report, the Council already provides on its website a significant amount of information, including financial and economic data used in the preparation of its annual reports and information about the basis for each of its designations of financial market utilities and nonbank financial companies. As a collaborative body that brings together the independent financial regulators, much of the data relied upon by the Council is provided by those agencies and the Office of Financial Research, which maintain the responsibility for determining whether to make their data available to the public. However, to the extent that the Council considers data and information during Council meetings, Council staff will routinely evaluate whether such materials could be made available to the public, in light of any applicable confidentiality restrictions.

Thank you again for the opportunity to review and comment on the Draft Report. We value CIGFO's input and recommendations and look forward to working with you in the future.

Sincerely,

Mary J. Miller

Appendix V: CIGFO Working Group

Department of the Treasury – Lead Agency

Eric M. Thorson, Inspector General, Department of the Treasury, and CIGFO Chair

Theresa Cameron   Susan Marshall

Jeff Dye   Maria McLean

Patrick Gallagher

Federal Deposit Insurance Corporation

Jill Lennox

Federal Housing Finance Agency

Tara Lewis   Andrew W. Smith

National Credit Union Administration

Marvin Stith

Securities and Exchange Commission

Kelli Brown-Barnes

Special Inspector General for the Troubled Asset Relief Program

Erika Szatmari   Porsha Brower